The Seattle Five Plus One

Sheila,
May the muse
jump off these pages
and bite you!

The Seattle Five Plus One

Poems by

Jo Nelson
Irene Drennan
Kevin Coyne
Priscilla Long
Jack Remick
Anne Sweet-Streeter

PIG IRON PRESS

Youngstown, Ohio

The Poets and Their Poems

The Poets and Their Poems

I
Jo Nelson

Tangle

Pale shades of ourselves,
we pick tomatoes by moonlight,
testing the ripe firmness of flesh
with half-blinded toes
echoing the wild geese
in the star strung wash of sagebrush
and a cricket lonely for fog.

Dew wet, morning breasts
heavy with scent of you
kiss skin electric -
a gray quilt struggles to tangle the sun
in your hair barely curling pillow,
arm fuzz circling my thigh,
your mouth slightly open
hums the hive of your eyelash brush
dawn birds temper the fights unspoken
lovemaking all the more deadly;
the wounding too deep to bleed
cocks crow a hasty race to busy
hens pecking at worms -
the bittersweet taste of hay washes over
the chill prickle the world
waits a dark steaming ripple
you must sip from a cup.

Penitentes

Mountains brood beyond shrouds.
Mud paths suck black boots along
tracks of ancient wagons
where wheels turned sand to stone.
Wind incants plainsong
crosses twist penitential
under the gaze of earth-worn gods.

Here no window eyes assign
souls of lone moradas;
negative stigmata oozing lack of light.
Inquisition superstitions
peel rigors from bare hills,
tear away the flesh of will
to bind with scabious night.

Beyond our hearing, a wolf-dog snarls
frenzied flagellations;
tongue and tail beat time
with the blood run rampant;
crusade lust thrust from death obsession
until the lamb of God slaughters itself
drop by silver drop.

Ojos

In Ojo Caliente,
sulfur corroded the air;
mud baths caked summer vermilion
but adobe soaked the wastes of old bones
gone for the cure
turquoise rimed in azure.
Madre de Dios
we prayed at the mission
robed in adobe still as the earth.
How can so much sunshine
grow chollo and sagebrush
skirt the red river,
the birds' willow flutes -
alkali veils became them -
Ojo minerale, Ojo de Dios
cure us, we pray
Ojo Caliente, Ojo de Dios
curanderos, curandarnos

Dias de Muertos

Osiris' death day
grown through Roman
flowers blossom with blood
Huitzilipochtli's thirst
for the cold flames
gravestones and butterflies
petal the doorways and copal
bears altars
bones sing backdrops the living play
dead share the fire warm
harvest thanksgiving
mummers join loved ones
graves light candles
knees mark with prayers
through sweet meats
of skeletons and skulls.

Mordida

Manolete dances the skulls
his ballet whirls a cape
horns rape sideways
the wind bows
his cape
a rage of bull tongues
screaming the blood death
muscles and hooves tap the dust
whirlwind he laughs,
the collective
breath crosses eye orbs,
holes in hands
the flash flesh
red piss and bull sweat
eye white in the circle
hooves paw
bone fingers twirling a cape
horns rake and toss
El/Asherah, Shiva-Nandi,
his hands raise invincible
steps hollow the blood road
horns impale the sky.

Ishtar Throws the Seventh Veil

By Babylon's bones I rest,
dream drugged and tear bereft.
No gardens hang the cascade fountains
air dried laughter hides in wind.
A dark cleft coils the spiral
virus of vines - the milennia
a night tomorrow swallows raw.
I join a juggernaut of lines, wailing
as the axe grinds life momentum down.
An arabesque of scarlet queues
the tensile sun flight
in whispers among the reeds.
Night scrolls old battlements;
lions prowl face carved lids;
myrrh and frankincense repent
unrelenting sand fall -
the water bearer's urns now empty
with the weight of years;
stars reel ageless scorpion trails
in the ebb and flood of blood tides;
the rise and fall of each new rule
placate time's tears.
Adad opens the floodgates,
the Euphrates silts another layer
over bricks turned to sand.
Wind tunes my lyre;
I rise, a new moon
to dance the death of Nebuchadnezzar.

Mark of the Beast

Suppose you deliberately shot your own brother
in the mountains on the way to a deer
what would Freud make of Cain detaining Abel all over,
Jake's blonde hair and your dark
herd on his land between you
though the father rage kept you apart -
he was twice your size
but his smile made him vulnerable
that morning fog climbed the ridge
where the deer tracks were cold
as your hands on the hammer raised a rifle
to the sound of a boot on a rock -
did you know as you pulled the trigger
you were aching to kill
your lust for his girl wife
wouldn't give you a nod
when the blood bloomed
your screams tore a hole in her
youth you forever forswore
your man face set in knowledge of sin
again and again you re-live that thunder
locked out of your mother's heart.
The judge at the inquest ruled it innocent
but his ice eyes knew your dark
and your father never said another word
but he threw away the deed
to the land
the brother blood on your hands.

Orpheus, Awake

How like Orpheus to guide Rilke's pen
in February when the earth seems dead
to the sun's touch
and sun itself feels wan
behind its forlorn mask.
Roses too are my metamorphosis
bound with roots and willow sap;
earth breath swings our sonnets,
plays the cobweb lyres
and the trees we've planted grow heavy
with the songs that snare their branches
to hold the star fires fast
so we who have tasted poppies with the dead
will tune our voices finite,
the two entwine more than one,
more than a wandering - a touch
earth bestows on farmers
as death refrains the magic spell;
the ring of bells we dance;
the measure of the earth
that throbs springing red
to awaken flowers
who know enough to bless their gods.

Violins and Moon Spin

The summer the gypsies lived at our farm
the air was warm with the laughter of rain
running violin yellow over red ribboned roads
Dad left Mom in charge of three boys
and me in charge of the chickens
while he went to Alaska for silver
for taxes and mortgage.
How he could leave us alone, I now wonder
with out-of-work men on the roam
but the gypsies came and saved us,
their horses all tassels and twirls
their wagons of flowers and rainbows
strung flames we sang at night after chores
danced open my wild fiddle heart.

Do-gooders sent the preacher out
to talk some sense into Mom
gypsies were no models for kids, he told her;
none of the good people wanted them around
they were probably in league with the devil, he said
but Mom held more truck in gypsies than psalms;
she ushered him right to the door
his cup of dark will still steaming the table -
religion turned Mom gypsy right there
she joined us at night by the fire
tied her hair with a blue silk ribbon
gifted rings of gold in her ears
danced to the wild violins.

Gypsy magic held sacred the female
and Mom blossomed under their care -
the grimmer the townspeople grew,
the more Mom sang and hoed turnips
laughed when she wrestled the plow
or hauled water to save the dry corn.

That summer the boys became men
changed by music and moon -
Pop brought back a blue-eyed dog
killed the pig we roasted by moonlight
an apple in his mouth.

Swallow

Mon petit oiseau, my little bird,
I hear her cricket whisper
the feather fold beneath my head
before the dreams claim me.
I feel the light bless of her lips
smell the ginger
soap her sisters sent from France.
The mistral stirs me;
je fais le pierrot qui, the fool
wonders why the mask does not smile
the way we willed it.
I hear her knees   crack,
feel her back stiffen mine
we are lost in a time people wander circles,
fairy rings frost the lawns.
Nous marchons comme le canard,
we waddle drunken paths through parks
that sleep winter's dark;
shadows brush the windows blind
before light breaks the mirrored
reflections sparrows spin.
The clock strikes a chord.
Tu jases comme un merle
she'd say and I did chatter,
my black hair against her china skin
we'd sit and drink *cafe au lait,*
the cups bone thin in our hands;
steam fogged her glasses
gray as the lake face sun struck.
We sat in the bay window

and she read ***Blanche Neige***
Une hirondelle ne fait pas le printemps
one swallow does not mean spring
and I wondered why her hands shook
at the telling;
why our eyes teared
before I knew life's fragile saucer
empties broken shells.

Lathered

It was the wind that spun us
wind that gored us dry
wash running sand
licked at sky
licked us black from the no-haze
buzzards picked with bone
culled from stare eyes.
It was the wind that sang our nether song
wind that raced dark paths along
wind that cast us
in the swirling foam lipped
dance the river longed.
It was the wind that rocked our foals
wind that held our wild-eyed
wind that raced white mares
down roads lined by tree crack
breath of hot wind on your neck
breath of fresh wind.

Asyntaxia

Catbirds in a guilded cage,
we take city words apart
rhythms open street sounds;
steel strings blossom rage
racing time against will
two/two; too too; tutu
the pavement
strings horn jazz beat
hot tar jive
bus door mannequins
Coca-cola stube step nobreath air
booming heart beat
white shirt
brief case no light
sixty hour work weeks
marble voices aca, aca
acappella.

Eating Up the Road

The Second World War force-fed America
with the cadence of the road -
fifty Chevys, big bumpered; hunkered down,
their fins and tails flailed
paths of black topped winding
Desoto / Ford grills grinning silver toothed
Crosleys and Henry J's made
forty-five miles to the gallon
with gas so plentiful, no one noticed
boys fresh off the farm
drank their cafe au lait; their vin ordinair
slouched toward Hollywood
pasteboard washed white homes -
all around those picket fences
love and rugs painted colors
film makers infected
the innocent way we saved
perfumed sex and rampant consumption
played full houses banks drafted
people to spend all their time
chasing dreams down the rolling endless
prairies and grain fields;
rivers muddy with cows
lined up the roads black and white
striped country towns
drowned in factory chic
when we bombed engines to overdrive
moving vans cruising the national
debt grew in proportion to automated
eating up the roadsides -
Boston Commons, the Loop, Saint Louis
arched the golden bay at San Francisco
aquariums flooded with angels
while the Valley grew poppies
and peach skin bikinis on rooftops
waited for the surf to rise.

Breach in the Wall of the World

Crickets rise against the wind moan
moon laces trees to silver grass;
blue horses part the owl scream
to feather fall bones rattled emptyfull;
crows draw blood mist from the crack
between dream sleep
feather fog muffles in quickening
water breaks
mud dams throb the salt rush
aligned in Orion's sheath.
The sweat agar
melds bones into a humming
that writhes root bound in sand
until wastes leak shadows
the fireball horns hollow
chimeras of water and dust -
we float the primordial
born again in nacre.

II
Irene Drennan

Pike Place Market Incident

Beyond winters improbable flowers
a garden of cabbages and crabs
where the sun no longer probes my shoulders
there is a stall of mirrors
I can not pass them by.
Who are these old women dressed in black
hair driven mad by the wind?
mirrors, mirrors full of crones
you can not slow my step
I shout
shake my fist
an orange
a rock
something round flies at the startled hags
the air fills with splintered glass
and shattered women.
I turn to run
confident of my escape.
I am young.

a winters night

out of the winters fury came a lunatic
unbidden to my door
saying

i am welcome here
i have just escaped my jailers
with songs no one can sing
but me
i live in a palace
the house of the bleeding red cross
you are the mother of girls
you are the mother of boys
you are my mother
st. theresa

she wore an emblem of everlasting life
around her throat
she asked for warmth
i sent her into the cold
my words streaming after her

get out
stay out
i am resident lunatic here

kerouac

i see you standing
outside the saloon
by the railroad tracks
fashion plate handsome
against skyscrapers
death watches you with affection
from the flat glass window
stalks you through alleys
in and out of bars
stirs your beer with bony finger
sucks your heat with tongueless mouth
races you home
sleeps with your wife
no need for cocks crow of steel alarm
you do not rest easy three in a bed.

"mamere" trembles in the kitchen
drops the eggs
her eyes glue to the sinister separation
that slimes across the floor.

the door bursts open
walls crack
plaster falls
a man in black picks letters
from the settling dust
i understand before he makes a word
you are dead.

Jack Remick

(bastard son of Baudelaire)

it's grey in hong kong
hotter than hell in arles
but somewhere in gorst
on a mescaline morning
under the foggy pines
a man wades through salmon streams
roping broncs in his mind
birds rain down
at the very first sound
of his metal metaphor
filled with thighs
and secret sighs
and rock bands gone berserk
a crazed bee full of wine
can you imagine the honey

we all sit on the silty shore
feet in cold green water
holding tight
bottles wrapped in paper

it's a daffy down trip
past sleeping ships
and gorstian witches
to that damp dale
where words swoop down like carrion bats
to mess with our heads
explode a confetti of letters
right there in the bastards bed
warlocks and witches
exchange ideas in the smoky dew
clothes long lost
in the weedy wash
no one can stop them
no act of god
no law of man
it's a bacchanal in the gorstian wood
under the foggy pines

the lower west side

where everything was done to music
and little girls played with chickens tied to strings
that disappeared somewhere in the dark
and watched big girls strut and fluff
hair like strawberry sherbet
like licorice
like autumn leaves piled high and ready for burning
on the steps of saint christophers
a girl pollutes the air with profanity
as she waves her unpaid bills
at the word wounded winos asleep at her feet
while i marched in protest parades
and followed tears into five and dimes
to buy post cards for friends
who like to think of me drinking tea
with pony tailed mohawks
before i went into late evening
to vomit words over the heads of tourists
for wine and spaghetti
and my nightly fight with an african poet
who confused his penis with the empire state building
erected for white girls only

i pressed against the older poets like a baby bird
that risks peck and claw for a little warmth
'til strong enough to leave the city
that followed me like a sound that needs no echo
and sent me highballing across three thousand miles
of hot hazy highways
back to the maze of cracked concrete

and wind washed graffiti
to stand alone
shouting
will someone
anyone
please welcome me home

lower west side 2

fourteenth street sweats
like a played out whore.
writers stone dead
after super duper tough work
taggin' 'cross town
in one night flat.
day shift pimps
restless as rabbits in heat
hip-hop to bone bending music.
hot-pops grin from brown stone stoops
altar sized crosses swing from their necks
as they hawk pubescent girls.
street walkers bless themselves
before climbing into limos or black marias
ask st. christopher for safe return
to their havens of herpes and hard liquor
where altars wait
candles lit
grateful to be alive.
blessed are they among women.

sometimes
when night turns ragged
nothing left to break
no one to curse
they hit the sidewalk
wishing they were old women
like those that line the pews
of corner cathedrals.
safe in the arms of Jesus
broken eagle weeping blood.

lower west side 3

i see it all
like a bird flying over dying trees
the short row of tenements
where dreams unravel
and love is lost in dry white time
the dove of peace shot by children
the guns on their hips are real.
a bloody confetti falls
pretty as pomegranate seeds
small fever on the landscape
dark calligraphy in my mind.
it's cain and abel
adam and eve weeping in hell.
people pray
words fall like rosary beads
said in penance
they beg
lick spittles at the Lord's feet.
what wild card brought them this
brought me
a dream warrior with one dream left
my guardian angel paralyzed with rust
panic takes me up
seven flights
close to heaven as i can get
stars are peeling from the sky
God is deaf
Christ is dead
resurrection ... a rumor.

W.C. Handy

I walk through a sick mix
of sunshine and wine smell
pass the apollo
cool womb that cradled Elvis and Ella
where young hopefuls are made and unmade
faster than beds rented by the hour.
A legend waits for me
I am honored.
It feels like stage fright only warmer.

I barely see the saxophones and flutes
greening like sausages in the dark.
The old man strums a guitar
my heart beat disturbs
the rhythm of his blues.
He stops to dish up butter beans and bacon
i wash mine down with kool-aid and gin
hoping i look seriously hip.
Feel guilty
a little foolish.
This blind exile from the past
soothes me with timeless calm.
We share the melody of pawn shops
and gather dust
the same as cellos and congas.

Summer days pass September
find me in a Harlem cafe
perched like a nervous bird
on a chrome and plastic stool.
Crows push upwind
small pall bearers too late for the funeral.
Red words reflect the gleam of trumpets
sound hangs
abandoned in the window
beyond the hope of open doors.
The waitress fills my cup...
It begins to rain.

midnight

we listen half asleep
in the middle of the night
as though underwater
to the music of old blues records
we realize
mid-chorus
the microphones have gone sadly crazy
and the music is coming through the charred skulls of
mice
pushing through windows of our own voices
and the cavities of a brass ax
trying to reach a savior
blinded by slivers of glass
a savior of the streets
a savior of pot
wine and loneliness
a red moon savior
who fights with violet violent stars
like alley cats in the navy night
we wake
to find ourselves dissolved in a neon womb
put up our hands and open our mouths
to catch an orphan down beat
is it morning yet

no dog days for me

arrows of geese shoot south
dead leaves dangle from the trees
I deny the cold message.
Autumn does not charm me
or heavens blue glass lie
that leads to winter thought
numbs my head
Empty nests watch
like the lonely eye of God.

Keep the green rim of time
that sucks the anger from my pain
fevered roses splashing perfume in the air
the tight line of crows
that circle the earth
reflecting orange landscapes
orange nights
orange dreams
hair blowing orange
sounding like drum songs and snake bone rattles
lullaby of hollyhocks
tough enough to bloom in city streets
unconcerned with the drab day
that will find them gone.
Stay the copper hour
it's these hard flowers
i want to keep.

psychedelic winter

the sky
blue and bland
smoothes their skin
eases the weight of age
legs
twenty summers long
step across time
to touch silver fountains
and dark bars
that smell of musk and promise
time splinters beneath their feet
a sun spun river in their veins
warming thighs
surprised by the unexpected spring
their life rewinds
the same flinty girl waits
in decades of psychedelic flesh
his cloudy music in her bones
glory to their ears
glory to their eyes
until they talk
until they drink brandy
until cold reality joins them
flattens the hour of their hoped for
longed for union

prayer for Sara

Jesu Christo
put a flower where a heart once was
in Sara made of stone.
She burns red and white
in ding-dong halls with iron doors
walks with angels
wearing halos of stained gauze roses
bleeding pink
stares into the terrible eyes of saints
and does not tremble.
Their sighs bring no relief
or even cool her cheeks.
She casts a double shadow
queen of all whores
nuns frown over her shoulders.
Jesu Christo
head twice bent
once in death
once in dust
she abandoned her beads
her rancid perfumes
blood streaks lightning across her shirt
her smile is pinned on with two small pains
nails pierce her nipples
curdles her human milk
she approaches you from all sides
why do You not see her?

Brian

The moon searched the black water
but you did not want to be found.
I knew where you were
when the angry ocean rushed the shore
to spit sharks into my garden
the air heavy as your broken promise.
We were to live among the tlingits
making snow men red with wine
but you are in the wet and weatherless
peace of green
where all private suffering ends.
I can see you deep within my mind
beneath the sea
where small fish play between your ribs
the bigger fish feast away your flesh
the anemones that sprout from your skull.
I can almost feel the seaweeds soft embrace
the heavy water that holds your body down.
Did some zealous priest cull your bones
and set your spirit free?
Where did all the tears go
after so much weeping
did they soak into the earth
dry up in the sun
or just run down to the shore
to put more salt into the sea?

Chinatown Moment

the old man threads his way
over spit dappled streets
coughs to expel the lie
caught in his red jelly entrails
looks through pox marked windows
at blue dyed ducks
pressed wing to wing
in porcelain pans
calling up gold fan memories
and flayed dreams
i stand close
his hair turns in my breath
i carry him in my mind
beyond piss damp alleys
where he smoked as a boy
the stall lined midways
where imitation guccis
and breeze battered t-shirts
are sold to tourists
who don't give a damn
about those behind doors
sealed with penny post cards
his face appears in the dirty glass
hovers over porcelain pans
i will remember him
long after the last duck is eaten.

Totems Wait

Beneath my feet
a bridge that spans reflections
covered with army blankets
stiff with dirt and crushed roses
thrift shop tickets
and bathrobes that bleed into the sea
a lone boy bathes
bits of glass cling to his skin
eagles wash their kill
count bones behind mirrors
I
held motionless by rusty razor blades
and old toothbrushes
watch spirits spark like fire flies
rush restless toward totems
closer and closer to the holy poles
where those who die free
dance in the no breeze hour
'til the warm lean of dawn
time to leave the gentle dead
re-enter the peopled morning
alive and free
totems wait

III
Kevin Coyne

My Three Nuns

I want to thank the nun
who stung my cheeks
a quick-draw slap
Three Stooges double whammy style,
the square edge of her palm imprint
hidden beneath this beard gone white.
She is the reason for my easy blush.

I feel a warm glow
for the one whose ruler
cracked its lightning across my knuckles
ten whacks for rubbing out
Wednesday's ashes. From her I learned
pain is measured in inches.

And thanks to the kind sister
who brought me to my knees
when I kept my dime
and put a button in the box.
Her vise grip fingers twisting my ear
taught me humility.

I'm grateful to these nuns
who hammered out the facts of life
amid the fiction of God.
From their nailgun cruelty
I acquired a love for slapstick
and a strong dislike for carpentry.

Communion

My father drops me
off at church,
then goes to get some
hair of the dog.

The bartender fills
an empty cup.
Dark wood, stale air,
smoke in the mirror,
whiskey on my father's lips.

The priest breaks bread,
consecrates the wine,
magic in a chalice,
Christ on my tongue.
Blessed be the father
and blessed be the son.
One seeks relief,
the other seeks redemption.
His light, liquid.
Mine, a melting host.
Flames trickle down our throats.

After church
my father picks me up,
Four Roses on his breath.
His face a mass
of broken vessels.
Mine, a mask of piety.

Purified, we head for home,
glowing in the heat
of our separate fires.

Comforter

The promised afghan
arrived today
in a box marked priority.

Opening it I'm struck
by the color of autumn leaves
on a wet New England sidewalk.

The yarn is natty and worn.
Loose threads cowlick,
tickling memories.
Odors drift across the years.
I drink the sudden scent
of Jean Naté, Tetley Tea
and a hint of cedar.

This is the comforter I used
for cover and concealment,
dodging the draft
winter 1970
Grandma Tin-Tin's apartment.

I found sanctuary on her couch
while Huntley-Brinkley
boasted body-counts
and broadcast
black and white the blood
of an undeclared war,
and the silent
scream of a young girl running
naked in the napalm.
I put the afghan back in the box,
the fabric too tattered
for comfort tonight.

The Mill

Summer's candle sputters down
the overgrown garden ripe.

Autumn simmers the wick
long, light shadow-shortens,
air rotting sweet decay.

Winter stretches, winter yawns,
hungry for bark, hungry for stone.
Time to pierce the pomegranate.
Time to let the red juice flow,
down the fiery sluice,
down through the sulfur stench,
down into the pulverizer
flesh and fiber, tooth and bone.
It's war again and again war
    thunder rumbling
    mortar shell shock troop
    blistered fields of fire
war stink-charred flesh
war machine gun staccato
war above the knee below the neck
    torso amputee
war white-hot machete
war cloven-hoofed jack boot
    broken rib and sternum
war sucking war chest wound
    purple hearts pumping down

the dead the dead the dead marking time
in never ending never again and again ever war.

Near Dead

The near dead dream
with rheumy eyes open,
pupils ceiling pinned,
peering into the vast vault.

The near dead mouth breathe,
tongues catching dry throats.
Their limestone lungs exhale chalk.
Their bones whistle empty white.
Their hollow veins echo the red sea howl.

The near dead hunger for death.
They choke on deathberry seeds
in the eyes of the living.

The near dead know futility of flesh.
They know how quickly time turns malignant.
They know the tumor swell and burst.

Underneath the star-burnt canopy
on slabs of granite the near dead die,
the dead make dead
love, and the living sleep,
coins on their eyes,
dreaming the dream of the dead.

Still Life

Helen lies in bed in a semi-private room.

A painting of the family farm hangs on the wall
above the blaring Zenith, where a white goddess
turns her letters and the wheel spins.

Helen was a farm wife. The homespun painting
done by her neighbor, lacks depth, but captures
midsummer. The mood is lemonade,
and the greens and yellows are sun-drunk.

The whitewashed house with tin roof
and blue trim whispers decades. Shade oaks
hover under cumulus. A red barn
runs to ground in the shadow gone scene.

Helen talks of the disappeared family farm,
auctioned off to pay for the room
she shares with Rose, who snoozes
during Bingo and reruns of Green Acres.

Helen did not want her children to be farmers.
One is a nurse, the other teaches.
They are close to retirement. They visit
everyday. The grandchildren work
for Microsoft. They visit when they can.

Helen lies in bed, her farm on the wall
collecting dust inside a weathered frame,
a frame built from remnants
of a hundred year old fence.

Helen, 86, lies in bed, a vanishing, point.

Night Watch

Two bells. In a hospital bed
bleached white, an old salt, skin taut
as mainsail with a bellyful of wind,
lies rusting twilight, undertow
flooding lungs.

Four bells. Tentacled ebb latches on.
Wind swings gale force, north-northeast.
Skeleton crews cast off lines
and tubes. The sleeping ship,
sheets to the wind, washes out to sea.

Six bells. Cross-currents clash.
Waves clap wet thunder.
Worm-eaten timber creaks.
Tendons tear
free in the rip,
muscle abandons bone.
The keel snaps,
the ribs collapse,
the bowsprit tips,
and the hull slips under.
Lantern fish light
down electric depths. Wrapped in rigging
the shrouded body corkscrews black wet,
wriggling into sand. Cell gives up marrow,
marrow gives up bone, bone gives up the soul.

Eight bells. Dead calm.

Sunrise

0640. End-of-shift.

Leaving the hospital I pass a co-worker,
Susan, cheerful and pointing east,
"Beautiful morning," she says.
Nestled in the cradle of the jagged Cascades
night hemorrhages into day
like a triple by-pass on a heparin overdose.

"You should write a sunrise poem," she says.

I look at the sky dripping red
and I see Herbert
wasting away from end stage Alzheimer's.
Plastic food in a kangaroo pouch,
via peg-tube, keeps him alive.
I hear the intermittent churning of the pump.

"I don't write about sunrises."

"I guess you're not a romantic," she says.

I get in my car, grateful
today is Sunday, no traffic,
and drive away
east, squinting in the fresh cut light.

I-5

High beams fire-up
your rear view mirror.
The passing lanes are empty,
but this jerk's persistent,
pointing his finger
like a stressed Uncle Sam:
he wants you,
his maniacal grin
menacing as the grill
on a '56 Buick.
You're doing the limit,
refuse to change lanes.
It's highway combat.
You hope he doesn't have a gun.
You slow down. He pulls around,
his arm reaching out,
aims, fires, and shoots you
with a gesture
meaningless from overuse.
He flies by,
disappears around a curve.
Adrenalin pumps your blood.
Heat floods your face.
You visualize him and his 4by4
French-kissing a bridge abutment.
Thirty seconds later,
there he is in the breakdown lane
pulled over by a trooper.
You cruise by at 55,
the blue light strobing
bounces off your smile,
a rush courses your veins.

Safeway

In the express check-out
you are an impulse caught in a trap,
smart shopper held captive
by screaming tabloid headlines.
MOM GIVES BIRTH TO DOG FACE BABY!
You stand there with your chunk light tuna
behind a dirty old man with twenty-three
cans of Vienna Sausage, seventeen packages
of Top Ramen, and three SlimJims
he pays for with foodstamps and a Social
Security check for seventy-five cents.
DR. KEVORKIAN SAVES WOMAN'S LIFE!
You notice the next line over is shorter.
You know better than to violate rule #1,
but you change lines anyway,
kicking yourself as the one you were in
shrinks and disappears.
OPRAH'S DIET SECRET? TAPEWORM!
People who were once behind you
are in their cars and on their way home,
and the checker calls a price check,
and the checker runs out of register tape,
and the checker leaves to get cigarettes,
and the checker counts a pile of ones
loses track and starts again,
and the idiot in front of you can't decide,
plastic or paper, and the lady behind you

bumping your butt thinks her cart is a plow,
and the checker cheerful, "Hi! How are you?"
is more than you can bear as a headline
blares, DOG FACE BABY ONE YEAR OLD!
You pull out a sawed-off shotgun,
pepper the dairy section with buckshot.
Broken eggs and Monterey Jack
omelette the floor. Two-percent milk
bleeds white. I Can't Believe It's Not Butter
splatters the walls. You swivel and pivot
and riddle the pickles firing from the hip.
Zeroing in on the herbal tea, you zap
the Red Zinger, put the Sleepytime asleep
and give the Morning Thunder
a wake-up call. On your way out the door
you pull the pin on a hand grenade,
John Wayne the Grey Poupon,
and then you remember,
"Damn! Forgot the Miracle Whip!"

Algebra

Math woman at her window solving for x,
looks up from her work and out at the crows
dancing and changing partners in her yard.
One crow, jealous, plucks a beakful of down
from another's breast. Math woman out
the door, scaring the crows, snatches up
the feather bouquet and lifting it to her face,
rubs the petals against her cheeks absorbing
iridescence. She plants a blood-filled stem
in porous rock. A shaft opens.
The quill leaks fluid, permeating magma,
and all the crows square and square and square
again, until a black cloud blankets
Earth's green bed. Everywhere crows peck
a hungry crawl earth turns to stone, crumbling
under crows' feet to dust. Math woman sneezes.
Tunnels implode. Gullets rumble
empty in the dark. Math woman at her window
whisking with a tail feather sun-colored hair,
whips the static around her head to a frenzied
phosphorescence. Swirling in the void, sparks
ignite, a bolt jumps free, streaks down,
carving a jagged fault in stone. A blade of grass
seduced by light, spears the night, while deep
within the fissure, a wrinkled pink unfeathered
head pokes up through the smoking crust.
Math woman, open to the wind, refigures
the formula. Fingers fluttering, she juggles
the equation, considers probability.
Math woman's window slams down,
glass shatters, shutters unhinge, black wings flap.
Math woman checks her work. The universe
bears down.

The Return

Bound to this rock
I wait while God midnight shadows,
then dips below the rim to winter.

I wait for God to icebreak,
to snap these chains,
to lead the way across the barren tundra.

I wait for God to thunder melt,
to grunt and belch,
to pick the righteous from his teeth.

I wait for God to lightning strike the frozen sky,
to fly the wind electric snow.
I'm waiting for God to slay this eagle,
to gut the night belly black,
to show me the place where dead crows go.

I'm waiting for God to juggle fire,
to flood the world with light and grace.

I'm waiting for God the prodigal sun.

Meditation On Monk

I first heard Thelonius Monk
before I could spell jazz. I could spell
rock and roll and Johnny B. Goode,
but jazz was confetti to my juke box ears.

Today I'm forty-six. The sound of Monk
on laser disc filters through
woofers and tweeters,
notes and chords condensing in a cloud of J-A-Z-Z.
I know as I listen to *Misterioso*
that I have lived my life tone-deaf,
thirsting for tonic the soul can drink.
I dig the Monk's Epistrophy
of off-center solos,
the sharps and flats of black and white equations,
and I can spell
jazz, I can spell
Bird, I can spell
Trane, I can spell
Lady Day, and I can spell
Mister Night with a shotgun in his mouth.

Today I scribble the walls of a cave, a Monkophile
dribbling dregs of one more *Straight No Chaser*
black with sugar clouds bursting jazz, Jazz, JAZZ
the blue rain, rhythm-sweet,
cool kissing soft flesh, cool licking every pore,
cool quenching the hungry heartbone.

Trench Mouth

Metallic breath of a new day
greets you in the morning
smelling of decay: red tide
creeping along the gumline
of incisor, canine, premolar, molar.
Only you and your periodontist know
the blood secret your mirror holds.
You would sooner tell your lover
you have HIV or herpes, than a mouth
that bleeds. When you floss, your fingers
flick red flecks on glass reflecting
the grimace of your fade to gray choppers,
some of them cracked, some of them crowned,
all of them drilled and amalgam filled.

You ignore the warning signs: the pink
brush and crimson froth of Tartar Control
Colgate sliming the bathroom sink,
symptoms of infection gone unchecked,
bacteria chomping away in bone deep hiding.

When these enamel soldiers
standing at attention on the frontline fall,
no sharp reserves erupt to fill the gaps.
No, these hardcore troops gone soft
and loose are inmates on death row, waiting
for a last meal before they're extracted
from their purulent pockets, pliers pulling,
scalpel scraping, and you inhaling gas,
laughter escaping your toothless head.

IV
Priscilla Long

On The High Cost Of Keeping Horses

In the black of night
I go down sleepwalker
down to dank cellars
damp the rotting stair
duck the danger beam
the rotting danger beam
down to hidden stalls,
festering hidden stalls
where stamps and snorts
my wild dapple mare.

We ride high the hot air,
clamber sky and cloud.
Her hooves pound my heart,
her neigh flickers hot joy,
haunches race and ripple,
nostrils flare.
The cities begin to burn.
Flame licks the hot body of the sky.
The sky shudders and sinks into tongues of fire
and the cities burn.

Like Certain Old Women

Autumn dances drunk.
Oxblood oaks sway and shake
naked their dark arms. Pear trees
burn to cinnabar. Sumac fire
licks the bronze evening light.

Clouds rustle the great maples
just to flutter their crows. Birch
leaves tumble with hawthorn haws,
chestnuts with acorns.

Nothing remembers its place.

Nuclear Winter

After that war, still
the tides will tauten
and slacken on the moon's rope.
The earth will turn, and turning,
snowpeaks mirror sunlight
in sharp blue mornings.

And there will be colors:
grey and white mist,
the old red sky at dusk,
the deadpan moon, and earth
everywhere blackened.
And, foraging on the ocean floor
among cave and cavern: enormous, eyeless
sea-monsters -- the word comes
from our storybook mind -- prehistoric
invertebrates that move
through human understanding
into the darkness beyond.

Snapshot: Seattle

The vise grip--unusually cold--
stirs the town to housetending,
to stuffing socks into sills

and jambs. We stove
our rooms, wrap pipes, stop
gapes and leaks,

nurse the old housebones.
The sudden freeze provokes
cheerful nesting noises,

house to clapboard house.
Done with pipes, we snug
with book, quilt, and cat. Downtown,

ice cracks brick and stone.
Three men sleep in bags. They stick
straight out, like three good

children all tucked in,
highrise for headboard.
Above, their flag is flying.

The cold stars shine.
They lie stick-stiff, and over two
breath whitens the cruel air.

Legacy

(Susanne Long, 1946-1986)

This year, sister,
I move to the green wet
of your Northwest,
by chance or circumstance.
These chill days of rain
I wear your purple coat
snapped shut. I splash
across your streets, breathe
your spruce and pine.
Your mountain rises still
in cedar-mist. I hear
the flap and caw of crows,
the cry of gulls. Puget Sound
is mine now. I have your voice
on tape, your photo
on my wall, its
ice blue eyes.

The Printer's Poem

Machine meter clunks
inside skull walls,
clanks printer's time
for words put one to one.
Outside, words pile up
in stacks of sheets.
One hundred parts are clicking
each to each. Cam followers spin
to whirl their spirals straight.
Gears turning gears
push levers up and down.
Each clack and whoosh
extends the human hand.

Here is history
cast in metal:
the wheel, lever, language,
fire changed to power. Lithography
keeps the old way of writing
words on stone. The printing head
presses thoughts on sheets, paper

changing to pages turning
in fingers, to words turning in mind.
A simple idea cast in metal:
that one idea repeated
a thousand times can stir
a thousand minds. Still,

a poet's heart pounds
to inside words.
They falter up
into industrial din
and drone, word
by single miraculous word.

The Return Of Geese

In the long, low loneliness of geese honking,
the river of darkness that bore me
from childhood returns tonight
and I wrap myself in the loneliness
that bore me here and I am
safe in the dark river of haunting
geese, the moonless night of dream
that carries me, rocks me
dreams me, child again in the arms
of darkness, safe in the honking
darkness, the river dreaming me
to shore in the darkness I love,
lonely the river of darkness I love,
alone in the river of darkness I love.

Seascape: Narragansett Bay
For M.K.

Beyond Monahan's Pier, the archaic moon
washes light across obsidian seas.
Foolish radios have faded to foghorns,
to white waves descending on granite
like great birds scattering. Night's
immense cave holds each gull, reed,
and stone. Among somber tones, we
are small, one two-edged stroke
along the seawall. Our salt blood
surges to the sea's roll. Salt wind
hollows us smooth, simplifies
involuted sands, castles of ambition.
We walk toward pier, rock, and foam
into darkness, emptied of ourselves.

Summer Nights

Rain dissolves this night's mind
into memory's dark river:

the green rain of the south
drumming the old farmhouse,
its crusted, chronic angers;
rain hushing my hopes,
my girlhood ripe
for city lights, the blues,
poets shouting the world's questions.
Rain drones my vague dreams
and love's flame hisses
on the radio.

Or, long after, I long grown
stone-hard, the bedsheets white
in the long dusk of summer rain
and I am drinking from love's sweet mouth,
the friend of my heart, our mother tongues wet,
dissolved into kiss, rain pounding
our hearts wild, hushing our sighs,

and after, the utter peace,
the perfect peace of rain.

The Light At Arles
(Bedroom, 1888, Van Gogh)

A stripped-down room:
bed, basin, board;
a poor man's clothes hung
on nails, two old chairs,
the sun-drenched afternoon
painted in a peacock century.

Soon the light will fade
to shadow, the bed to shape
and color of sleep.
Soon Munch will carve
his scream. The century will die
into its pictures.

Later, the Great War.
Nothing simple, nothing
filled with light.

Peacock feathers will scatter,
overstuffed chairs leak bugs
and batting, bric-a-brac break,
old realities disintegrate.

Only this remains:
the bare bone of dream,
a narrow bed, essential
rooms dim-lit by inner light.

Abstraction
(after Mark Rothko)

Grotto of sleep, dark,
not black but soft,
deepening to violet
below dream, to underwater
cave, imageless, edgeless,
the dream of not
dreaming, floating
in corporal darkness,
down below down, a weightless
weight, the self dissolved
in a sea change, strange
caverns gathering night.

Realms Of Desire

Deserted cobble streets winding
in fog, past crumbling stone
walls, old gardens, Biblical
olive trees twisted intimate
through time-ruined years . . .

Fog drifting blind in stone streets,
stone steps worn smooth
as skin, air light as breath,
light as nothingness, eternity
winding through summer days like fog . . .

A stone rune scratched obscure
as unremembered dream.
Objects of desire: old clocks,
wood-carved cogs of waterwheels,
a locked box, a time-pocked face.

Images shift inconsolable.
Yearning drifts thick in dubious streets.
The god is nameless,
the temple in ruins.
The throat aches incantation.

Rhapsody

I walking fast under hot yellow skies,
the hot yellow fingers of the sun
stroke lightly my neck, my arms,
my salt-sweat face, stun the crows
silk-black and still. The wires sing,
the cars shining hot sing, the sand-hot
pavement sizzles and I sing the asphalt,
the steel-hot bridge, the blue lake,
white sails dazzling the dark
below the bridge. The sun hot
all in my hair tickles my arms,
tickles my back, tickles and strokes
my salt-sweat face. I sing
the black-silk road, the wires,
the creosote poles, the cars shining
past. I sing the ducks, the burberries,
the burgundy-dark trees. I walk
under hot yellow skies, the sun hot,
its fingers all yellow in my hair.

V
Jack Remick

Memory of Wood

Trees are bones of the killed land
bones scattered like lost children on the banks
of mud creeks under gray skies
bones of time in moonscape wasteland
of roots whitening in soil sterilized by profit
of roots holier than the bones of saints
roots shrivel into cracked tangles
and stumps probe for their phantom limbs
enshrined on Elm Street
I walk through the slain forest
through the bark stripped from trunks
through two by four rows of the dead
without markers or headstones
in the bedroom my fingers touch an inlaid box
an oak branch carved into a jewelry tomb
there is no sky here
in the spackled ceiling a nostalgia
of stars ignited by 100 watt bulbs
and in the corners of the living room
I hear a chorus of cries from picture frames
an oak floor elegy and I look
for the war-wounded blind
but see portraits of corporation
presidents in suits and ties
Creaks rise from the floor where I walk
the chairs and tables shriek
the house, dried skin of once live wood
speaks to its dead contains itself me
a veneer chest flayed skulks mute
against the plasterboard wall
it cannot see the ruin
though some memory must remain
of roots and leaves and slaughter
and blood from a ripped out tongue

lovdeth

I am in exile from your touch
as though I were dead were I dead
this agony finds its explanation
while you remain your eyes grace
other windows than my eyes where
there are no flowers of spring
no sweetness rains off your fingers
on flesh become a desert
this winter chill kills with a cold
so deepcold I die white blooded
what used to bind us blinds us
the habit of having days run by
without love running from your mouth
that once overran with passion
made us accept lovdeth
it is now late too late
and loves bones lie scattered

Beckett's Boils

Boils broke out on Samuel Beckett's neck.
rings of god-fire seething
out of the one word mouth
NO
Beckett's boils kept him awake
and awake he dreamed of a flat land
where thin men waited under leafless trees
where garbage can men lived buried
to their hollow eyes scouring
the flat land where Beckett
one man in gray wearing too tight shoes --
-- bunions and boils said -- fire, oh the fire
I want
I want - not
I will
I will - not - go
the flat land ate him chewed him into joycean
dust and he staggered on boiling feet
his mouth full of
NO
fingers running a rosary of boils
fire searing until Sam
moaned a mouthful of anger
crushed bringing Suzanne -- married years
to pain and silence -- out of her bed
angel fingers salving his crusted lips
cracked and dry speaking to the glass
    DUST, he said
Beckett dreamed lost in the dust
spreading in his vision
the line is gone now he said
broken the flow the mole of god
burrows to my surface on my tongue
in pustules the plague
I am - not
I want - not

I will - not love
anything but fire and torment.
on a flattening plain Hammer and Clou
nails driven into the skull
buried in garbage cans on a stage
where nothing happens twice
and always forever nothing
Oh happy days the sweet mouthed morning lays
its coated tongue on a parched
boil and he cries out the words
I will-not
and each will-not
births another volcano on his neck
his ear his eye his lip
but still he hears he sees he says
    I WILL - NOT
beg for deliverance from the empty flat
boils break out wild fire eats
his want-not do you want?
I will not
    BEG
I do not
    BEG
I will not
    PLEAD
I cannot
    PLEAD
I will not have not am not

He lies in the cold compress
Suzanne's eyes hollow hungry
Say it Sam she whispers licking her lips
    RAIN
Sam groans and thunder breaks
out of his agony growing words
little men waiting under leafless trees

Giacometti stick figurines waiting
for the kiln for the ovens for Dachau
empty eyed women in buckets full of dust
sing the one word song
NOT
NOT
modulating to
NO
NO
NO
I will - not
I do - not
I can not
BEG
and always in the dark pit, the fire.
Vanity, saith Joyce, vanity.
Why *do* you wear tight shoes, Sam
and tight pants, Sam
and tight coats, Sam
and why do you smoke, Sam?
And Beckett said
I - do - not - know
I - do - not - know.
And one day in Dublin under blue skies
his tongue sweet with Irish ale
he almost smiled and God said
    I WIN SAM
Beckett's boils came up a poison
sea eating his skin
an army of worms
eating his skin.
Beckett's pain was a labyrinth of night
and thin men and leafless trees
men full of hunger and sleepless nights
of dream-words

NO
NOT
NADA
NIHIL
NIENTE
NOTHING

And why Mr. B, do you wear tight pants?
Beckett smoked his Gauloise
I do not know, he said.
Little men waited under leafless trees
for shade and the word
that he will not
cannot
give to them.
Suzanne churned the dry plain
of a silent love with words --
Do - You - Love - Me, Sam?
Beckett smoked his Players
I do not know, he said.
Lucia, James Joyce's daughter,
hanged herself with words --
Do you love me, Sam?
Beckett ducked his wet lipped Gitane
in an ashtray in James Joyce's living room
and Samuel Beckett said,
I do not know,
I don't,
I do not know.

Prince of Burn

I am the prince of burn
aching for fire
acid batteries crack
holes in the world
sirens hammer the grind
me down to my knees
looking for a door
I feed my arms to snakes
I'm 22 but who gives a shit
I want to see the towers burn
to hard rock ash.
hungry eyed for fire
I sleep on stairs
under block letter signs
no sleeping
no living
closed keep out
I don't give a shit
curling up under the freeway
like a hungry dog
I inherit the holes in my shoes
I am a prince of parks
the king with the axe
the queen of hearts
the boy whore
I'll work for a dime
I see what I will be
by where I've been
I am the honey haired dream prince
superboy in flame-proof jeans
tomorrow I'll rise out of the night
in a black-eyed mask
with a gas can in my hand
I'll tag the message on your chest
burn burn burn burn burn

Coyote

they've kicked out my teeth
I don't sleep anymore
the weather rams
a storm down over the mountains
driven by wind into rain
thunder the grindstone
of earth takes the edges off the sky
sliding under the rumble
I hear coyote talk up on the ridge
telling the kids tales of shotguns
and poisoned meat and foot traps
they yip and yell, their primitive poetry
makes the hair stand up
on the back of my neck
it's a mystery I understand
primal voices in harmony
six point harmony, four fang harmony
tooth and claw counterpoint
laid down over a melody
of bounty hunters
and poison traps and plows
coyotes figure odds
better than a new york bookie
they sing opera you won't hear
at the met and the lyrics go:
okay, you bunch of bastards
run with us, see if you can keep up
nail this hide to your wall
I know I'm in the wrong race
I look at the sky and thunder
what happened to my blood
that ran wild and said screw you
to the bankers and the builders
I need to get back up there
on that ridge and howl at the plow
the bounty hunters and the poison in my gut

Light

this is the way i saw light
when i was a kid
the summer sun ran
off the walls of our white-washed house
it scalded the dirt
my brother and i walked
barefoot on the yellow line
to the river and back
the light in the asphalt
gnawed into our soles

when we played too long
without our shirts
we peeled slabs of us
dropped them on the ground
snakes in molt
the sun inside us
wiggled out
in the garden the sun
sucked water from the gourds
until they got crisp and hard
we made them into rattles
we shook like castanets
flamenco artists
and the sun in the seeds
slam-danced against the dark

autumn light was quiet
it spawned foggy mornings
chickadees sang to the mist
and spiders tied trees together
with silk
my brother and i watched
those webs wet with dew

we saw insects in straight jackets
and wondered how they heard
the sound of the jaws in the web

winter light was thin stingy
it stretched tight across the sky
we barely felt it on our backs
before it abandoned us to shiver
the walk home from school
feeling shadows in our coats

in spring new green dripped off the leaves
we found light splashed on the ground
it writhed in the purple flesh of iris
and tulip froth
it had pulled crocus out of the bulb
then anchored itself to the roots of trees

Jimi Hendrix Sings Purple Haze

we got naked and ate hash brownies
and listened to Marjo preach
we ate brownies
and tripped inside Ginger Baker
riffs that curled your
teeth
out of your
gums
and in my pad
with its black light
and a mattress on the floor
and six dozen yogurt cartons
spread out like meadow flowers
in a sacrificial field
we rolled in crisco
and listened to Jim Morrison
break his mother's
heart
and we smeared wheat germ
on alfalfa sprouts
and the food tasted brown
everything was good for you
but some things you didn't swallow
even if the books said it was okay
and we heard Janis Joplin
tear her
throat
apart chord by progression
down to ground zero
we were naked and high
on rope sized joints of colombian red
and then one night it ended
in the Haight on Scott Street
with a bad bunch of percodan

and the San Francisco mime troupe
improvising stoned naked
except for the masks,
but nothing masked the joints
and the dead boys
on the beds upstairs,
arms
still spiked
and we were still naked
but now rolling in
 blood
all the way to Woodstock
all the way to Altamont
where mafiosi with big
 grins
sold baggies of paraquat grass
to girls with long hair and no shoes
girls who ate pills of cut glass
and said mama where am I as they
bled to death
after Altamont we got our jeans back on
and half conscious rode herpes
in on an
orgasm
that lasted ten years
and left us pissing blood
we smiled
and said I suppose it was worth it baby,
I'm glad I did everything and I'd do it again
but why does it have to hurt so much?
we pulled on t-shirts with our jeans
and put the mattress up on a wooden frame
and put the yogurt cartons in the recycle bin
and unpacked the Brubeck and got cool again
and smoked strange tasting Marlboros
with nothing but tobacco in them

and we ate chocolate cake off plates
drinking our fears out of coffee cups
as we checked each other over
hands probing in rubber gloves
for hurt and the pinhead scars
and then, and then we put on hats
and london fogs and went to drink bourbon
and water in bars beside the still juke box
where the music had stopped
but the records
went round and round
I remember Jimi, I was there, I remember Jimi.

Jesus Christ Mother Gash

I am lost in the middle zone
blood filled with crystal
my bones crack muscles rattle
I feel "pig-eyed" a hog wild snorting rutter
I smell the shit in the raw red air
and sleep on the pain hardened sidewalk
eating the leftovers of the industrial love
affair rejected by my bosses
who stole everything that crawled on the street
where little boys selling chicle chicle chicle
say are -- you sick -- and point
at the tattoos on my arms

I am the corrupting angel of the dark city
soaked with the semen and sweat of thyroid dreams
where death worms deep in the skin
where needles of glass inject
me with diesel aids on the fly
where midget death cries open up
I need a heart to rest in
but I resist slam against the bar
cry no no leave me pass me by
go eat my brother mother sister aunt leave me
but needle death drives into my lungs into my eye
and I spread out belly weeping wet to my knees
spiked to the floor with christ's fingerbones
and then I see him

Jesus Christ on a barstool
Jesus Christ drinking boilermakers
Jesus Christ lord of snakes
Jesus Christ lord of crosses
Jesus Christ lord of worms
Jesus Christ blonde in black garters
Jesus Christ flashes her cross legged mother gash
bikini dress legs slick like salmon skin

her teeth dig the saliva from my mouth
she whispers stroke the mother swell of my breast
Take me, I'm what's left
I'll bury you in my blood and my bone
on my knees I taste the honey of his thighs
and he comes   moaning   yeast mold
on his tongue and grapes in his eyes
and I say am I saved am I saved am I saved

Osiris of Orchards

My roots are in the dust bowl
where my grandfather spat
Day's Work into a can
as he watched the horizon
for winds that blew his seed away.
My father, a young pariah hiding
from bulls in the belly of a train,
saw the land unfold and wondered
why his dreams had been eaten by dust.
Those winds did drive him westward.

Often he lay down in darkness
not knowing if he would rise.
He became faceless under his cap
tracking dusty vineyards
his ache melding him
into Every Man, an Osiris of Orchards.
The light in his eyes turned dim
and he, in angry emptiness,
did not envision offspring who one day
would call his troublesome times
past and not understand his sorrow.

And She, my mother, sprung first flesh
from generations whose sweat made earth
gush forth, whose human trees
peopled the prairies
she endured, with the patience all of you
my kin, have known, the hope
born of waiting for grain.
The winds have died down back there,
I do not venture back there,
the roots have shriveled
my grandfather is dead,
his seed growing in this place
where I will be forever.

Root of the Hoard

My dark-guard is being born into this tongue.
Words rise a bulwark of ancient rhythms
Casting shadows huge upon and over fear.
All it is will make me, and I am instrument,
Refined and honed now flesh-fish sharp,
Horde-hammerer, Shaper of the Unheard.
What is mine is not mine, but power given,
Crafting in me, entity of crush and build,
Sweep of swallow-singing and bardic froth
Gushing forth like blood from my word-wound.
I am rooted in this tongue -- the angle-image
Through me seeking light and sound
Leaps up, a dragon from centuries gone
As I grow wings, saxon-son civilized
By cogs, wheels, living in sky-needles.
Now, using this laser of the mind, I carve
Word-roads through the universe of rime
Creating spirit-maps of labyrinthine coil
And claim the treasure locked within those cells.

VI
Anne Sweet-Streeter

Three Sisters of the Crow

Crow crone dips in the iron
pool of sister eyes
and crosses sweet river of reed.
Thistles plucked
drift into the float downstream.

Owl brother hunts silence into dusk.
His yellow bladed beak
pierces robins blood breast.
Raven mourns
the coffin winter rakes over him.

Hag crow with cracked jaw,
constant sister of the tell all,
roosts on the bank
of her black forgiveness.
Hunched half-moon into belly folds
she drinks winter's brown fog.

Twilight sister calls,
Follow, follow.
Our bird blessings
water the silent soil,
fallow fragments of rock and bone.

In thickets of no light
crow sisters tip their heads
and sing through blue throats.
Sky teeters on their vacant call.

Mammogram

Waist-naked
against machine cold
the tech warm-handed arranges
flesh of my fear
flesh scared answer
that poison lumps have eaten
the flesh of my youth,
mammaries for babes
I have not yet had.
What if they arrive to lakes empty,
rivers dry,
the wild game gone,
fled south when fungus tainted leaves
twist and turn brown,
grass burned in the no rain sun,
limbs empty,
gnarled cores
waiting to blow loose.
Year to year
my flesh spread
passion bruised
suckled between plates
counting the times teeth
hard and white
have sunk into brown nipples,
panting caught on film.

A form letter arrives
bearing oranges and pears sent
from a place in the sun,
fungus halted by sterile note,
a mail order gift,
non-poison fruit
you will lick with your tongue
watching for lumps with your lips,
tasting again my fresh flesh.

Snake River

The river runs red with salmon.
My river runs red,
fertile drops that spread
through a tapestry of months.

Snake River telescoped reveals
a swim upstream against backwash,
the leaps,
the eyes tearless,
the noises of so few
unheard.
This year the count of one male
and one female
draws a bead through the gun sight of my mind.

So many eggs spawned,
washed downstream.
My river runs out.
Whispery are the thoughts I cancel
that this is
may be
the last run of salmon
through the mouth of my stream.

Sand Dune Walkers

From a photo by Edward Weston,
Dunes, Oceano, 1936

Dune walkers climb ripple carved sand
shackled by wind.
Broken against the blue black night
they climb, they fall, they crawl
hands blistered,
knees bent
against the down drop sand.

They came
night air mosquito thick,
journeying through wounds bleeding
with pinion and pine scrub
away from tall building night life,
blue time sign clocking their stay.

Neon thorns cut their scalps.
In crown throb sweet wet
they came,
came to climb the desert high,
saguaros touching moon
bent to sweeping sand.

Porous drains mean
through burned feet
and with loins on fire
they walk naked into thorn trees.
An eclipse darkens the sky
with their heat scream.
Purified and sun-baked
they pry their escape,
red eyes blooming at dusk.

Mozart Piano Quartet

Cello, violin, viola
spread my pores,
piano pulses
the heart beat
rhythm that bursts
as logs on fire.
I burn,
breath the smoke
of four men bowing,
bodies bent instrumental.

Four men thrust and heave
the fiery way men move
when they mount their women,
weave their love
with strings and ivory
pushing away the sheets.
I watch them spew
the milky cream
of clustered chords,
writhing pauses
over breasts hard
in the wash of viola.

Dazed
I guard against
the wild slipping in my mind
off their hands,
the wild I dare not touch.
Fire banked,
the curtain drops.
Spent and sticky
I stand, beating my palms,
the taste of warm fish on my tongue.

Violin

I am master only of the skewed rows of purple iris
at the moment I plant them.
Thread follows a needle
through a silk sleeve.
Violin,
tears drip from your strings.

When art has found its breath
in the hand of the artisan
the hoax most cruel is this:
When applied to canvas
winter melts.
Violin,
touch one single snowflake
wet to my cheek
and I will sing you iris dancing.

The taste of power fades
in the robes of concubines.
Their pinings lick seductive
at the navels of mongrel kings
who wretch the poet's plumes of conceit.

Violin,
cement laden hearts crack
when your melody lands.
I crave the words that
open the throats of mannequins
and turn papier-maché faces to flesh.

Shamanic Eye Echoes

In Montana
I found arrowheads,
stone and earthsmell.
I remembered a shaman's eyes.

Out of his eyes
beaver flow from dams
and the cave mouth
of his elk mother
breathes out brotherson,
swallows daughterfather.
Nostrils snort disease
tread in on boot heels.

Pox blankets snowwarm
wrap white
the wings of geese.
Parchment lips
search for buffalo water,
cough blood,
blow in the wind.

Beaded in shell and onyx
his magic rustles,
caught in the throat of fall.
He spits out songs
stripped of bark.

When I see
his eyes empty in me
he speaks cliff edged
to sky.
Wolf, his dog guide,
hollow howl opens the night.

Pregnant with Poems

Powder dusts moonsilver
temples that ache.
She twists
a thin tube of lipstick.
Fuchsia edged
her voice spills,
melts the heavy hand
laid on her thigh.
Her child poem
drops its head,
dilates her mind,
urges her to lay back,
spread her legs,
and push
through lips that rupture
cherry blossom bones.

Beach Prayer

Praying like a motherfucker
I kneel in gravel,
beach sea bed,
washed up storms.
I lean over,
cup seablue crystals,
pure baptismal memory splashed
on a white clad babe
by the hand of god presumed.
I kneel on gravel
self-splashed,
self-healed,
self-baptized
against storms brutal
the laugh of gulls,
angels above my head.

A motherfucker on knees
praying,
the uneven crunch of stones
smooth and round
slide away.
I move further down
into kelp and eel grass,
their stain breaches
the seasong wail
of orcas and otters.
Dead jellyfish slime
the in and out surf,
the callous tide
leaves and returns
used condoms and coke cans,
the unholy worshiped holy,
the prayers of a motherfucker
left cold.

The Barmaid's Story
(For Anita Hill)

I.

Ale flowed free in steins,
innuendoes honey thick
on her half-bare breasts.

She told of a prince.
From his mouth popped a fish.
His purple heart enraptured her.

The pythons stirred
         hissed.
They saw her honeyed breasts bare,
         appled.
They did not recall
the sunrise in her eyes.

She spoke all day his words,
silver-skinned words that smelled.
His purple heart enraptured her.

They emptied their steins,
clawed at her apple breasts,
licked apple flesh from their nails,
asked why
his purple heart enraptured her.

She couldn't say why --
he was a prince that smelled
of silver-skinned fish.

II.

Her eyes
the sunrise he saw
when he surfaced
to feed on flies
above the slippery waves
his prey the flies.
He the prey of eagles
a feather floats
from passion lofted.
He drowns in the mundane
he seeks to crush
with untruths
vulgar stories of rape gone bad.
Eagle man reaches inside Eagle woman
the barmaid virgin he kissed
silver lipped
behind closed doors
no one to confirm or deny
the fishery of sliming
through wet reaches of conspiracy.
He blinded her with stars
silver skin reflected.
She wrote angled stories
of deeds bent on raising
the eyebrows of his peers
while he hid behind rock
caressing her applehoney breasts.

The day she told
he leapt from surface water
eyes blazing the truth sunhot.
His purple heart.
She enraptured

by deeds hidden in kelp.
Eagles mate
their plunging ritual ends
a breath above the blue water
tumble to triumph
feathers fall to his reach
like flies at dusk.
His airborne leaps touch only
the lips of her sunrise eyes
his fakery not the victim
he preyed for.

After Reading
The Autobiography of Malcolm X

When big dogs fight
black and tan torn
by white tooth
next to embers low
the once fire dying
under sky black
stars thrown out
the scattering
of bird crumbs
hiss the evergreen boughs
laid on coals hot
and the black dogs growl
the one humbled
the other's spartan dew
collects on rock.

Franciscan monk
black and tan
swallows the dew from
white toothed Christian mothers
who taught we are
brothers born from the same bitch
or not at all
Taught
night cries outside the convent wall
are wolves after scraps
thrown out to keep them at bay
Dawn he looked
for prints
their near thrill danger
dissolved under villagers
who walked the night.

The lying hearts of motherguiders
taught what they believed

the choke right catechisms
the separate ceremonies
the caring pretended at him
His boxed ears
deadened the growling silent
the question in his eyes
The followed rituals
the words said right
the meantnothing words
said right
kept the outside wolves at bay
the hunger they chewed
the white punctured holes
A growl lows its way up.

The big dogs growled --
it was Christ
Christ spoke --
it was Buddha
Buddha spoke --
it was Allah
Allah spoke --
and the wolves outside
were in him
were him
humbled all that he knows.

Spider Woman

Spider white woman
blows discordant strings,
her jagged jazz harp billows the wind.
Webweaver catches light fire,
forests of dreaming.
Dew frozen crystals
touch ground against hard.

I brush away this webacross
with wind-broken branch.
She mends arhythmic,
trumpet lips
between bass finger tips.

White web
mother web
hangs in morning wet light,
sticky mock of maple sap
spilled raw.
Fir tree banjo dries by day,
trills daffodil horns.

At night her full moon rises,
gnats and flies wound tight
string from her pouch.
She bites the flagging wind
and reeds vibrate her teeth.

I stumble
chirping cricket notes.
She wraps me in white
and covers my face with her cloth.
She eats the brown spill
of my fern spore.

Sky Pony

The tone-deaf sky
bends me
with shortened days.
Icicles freeze
the prairie mane of a storm,
trees bridled in white.
Hooves paw silver against greyblue,
log cabin spell
of bleak waiting for wagons to pass,
spinning wheel echoes.

I weave a braid of hair,
knot, unknot,
knit barren the days.
Smoke chimneys
in the back up wind,
hour, long hour
smoke of a husband pipe
randy for spring.

Bear lumber from caves.
I emerge slow,
yeast rises warm before bread.
Yellow-breasted birds chick
in the dee dee sun.
Frogs cough in a pond
phlegm thick with croak.

Glove drops my wintered hand
on dry ground, I ask for rain.
Rain will come,
I ask for sun.
Sun will come
cut and laid in the field.
I ask for wind-dry hay,
but the black sky colics
and cows hunch against
the pony wind.

Chorus Line

Chorus girls bob beatwise,
dark-haired,
arm pit to arm pit,
in long-legged lines,
all the same namelessness
built up in their faces.
Their cast iron consciousness,
eighteen all-legs-one
catapult my daydreams sideways.
I do not try to escape.
I try to think their samethoughts,
their Catholic school girlthoughts,
but my rough edges
scrape at their bare thighs.
I bow apologetic genuflections
and wish I had not touched them.
Martyred stillborn children
are they real?
or wind-up representations
of coalesced fragments
of the massive oneness of us all?
If for only just one misstep
I could count the separate beats
of their heartthrobs.

Stiletto-heeled women,
they have kept to themselves
in their own same way.
It is the way each their dust has settled
that makes them whole
and alone.
Dust finds all the small differences.
I lean close
and carefully
do not breathe it away.

The Poets

Jack Remick has been a tunnel rat, social worker, community activist, bus driver, retail clerk, and college teacher. He is the author of a novel, *The Stolen House*, and *Terminal Weird*, a collection of short stories.

Priscilla Long is author of *Where The Sun Never Shines: A History of America's Bloody Coal Industry*. Her fiction and poetry have appeared in "The Southern Review", "Cumberland Poetry Review", "Southern Humanities Review", and elsewhere.

Jo Nelson is a Writer-in-Residence for the Washington State Arts Commission. A former bookstore owner, she now sells real estate and antiquarian books from her small farm in Gig Harbor where she also writes. Her poems and stories have appeared in anthologies and magazines nationwide.

Irene Drennan began writing and reading poetry in Greenwich Village saloons. She later graduated to the Sons and Daughters of Dementia workshop and founded the radio-poetry show *Zounds*. She is a winner of the Louisa Kern Award. She has a video, *Irene Drennan, City Poet*.

Kevin Coyne, winner of the 1992 Last Poems Poetry Contest from *Sub-Terrain Magazine*, has been published in *Mediphors, Exhibition, Pig Iron, In Your Face, Poets On:* and other magazines. He works as a night nurse in a Seattle hospital.

Anne Sweet-Streeter is a graphic artist as well as a poet. Her work has appeared in Pocketful of Dreams, Australian Wellbeing, Talking Raven, and other magazines. She received honorable mention in the Washington Poets Association William Stafford Competition in 1990 and 1993.